MW01529302

Mysterious Encounters

THE DEVIL

by David Robson

KIDHAVEN PRESS

An imprint of Thomson Gale, a part of The Thomson Corporation

THOMSON

★

™

GALE

Detroit • New York • San Francisco • New Haven, Conn. • Waterville, Maine • London

THOMSON

———————✦——————— ™

GALE

© 2008 Thomson Gale, a part of The Thomson Corporation.

Thomson and Star Logo are trademarks and Gale and KidHaven Press are registered trademarks used herein under license.

For more information, contact
KidHaven Press
27500 Drake Rd.
Farmington Hills, MI 48331-3535
Or you can visit our Internet site at http://www.gale.com

Picture Credits:
Cover: photos.com; © Alley Cat Productions/Brand/CORBIS, 16; © Archivo Iconografico, S.A./CORBIS, 27, 30; © Bettmann/CORBIS, 18, 24; © Historical Picture Archive/CORBIS, 38; © Francis G. Meyer/CORBIS, 21; Hieronymus Bosch/Bridgeman Art Library/Getty Images, 15; French School/Bridgeman Art Library/Getty Images, 12; Francisco Jose de Goya Lucientes/Bridgeman Art Library/Getty Images, 36; Paul Hawthorne/Getty Images, 28; Bernard Hoffman/Time & Life Pictures/Getty Images, 19; Raymond Medici/Getty Images, 5; Skip Brown/National Geographic/Getty Images, 10; Alberto Pizzoli/AFP/Getty Images, 40; Stockbyte/Getty Images, 6; Arthur Tilley/Getty Images, 9; Charles Walker/Topham/The Image Works, 33

LIBRARY OF CONGRESS CATALOGING-IN-PUBLICATION DATA

Robson, David.
  The Devil / by David Robson.
    p. cm. — (Mysterious encounters)
  Includes bibliographical references and index.
  ISBN-13: 978-0-7377-3780-6 (hardcover)
  1. Devil—Juvenile literature. I. Title.
  BF1548.R63 2008
  133.4'2—dc22
 	
                                                                2007022221

ISBN-10: 0-7377-3780-8

Printed in the United States of America

Contents

Chapter 1

SIGNS OF THE DEVIL

In 1975 a young woman met a dance partner she could not refuse. It was Halloween night. Customers at San Antonio's El Camaroncito Night Club were enjoying a spooky party filled with food and festivities. The dancer, whose name remains a mystery, was approached by a handsome stranger and asked for a turn around the dance floor. She agreed and offered her hand. There was something intriguing about the man. With his slicked-back hair, dark glasses, and crooked smile, he was somehow familiar to her. But she could not put a finger on it.

The music began and the mystery man began strutting his stuff. He had all the right moves. His smiling partner was flattered by his attention.

"But something strange happened when they were dancing,"[1] says Texas historian Docia Williams. As the music played, the friendly dance became a kind of hypnotic trance in which the dancer began to lose herself. Suddenly, she looked down at the floor. "Your feet! Your feet!"[2] she shouted. What she saw astounded her. Sticking out of the mystery man's pant legs were large chicken feet, a known sign of the devil.

The young woman screamed for help. By the time the other partygoers reached her, the stranger had disappeared.

The devil is often described as having a long tail, horns, and cloven hooves.

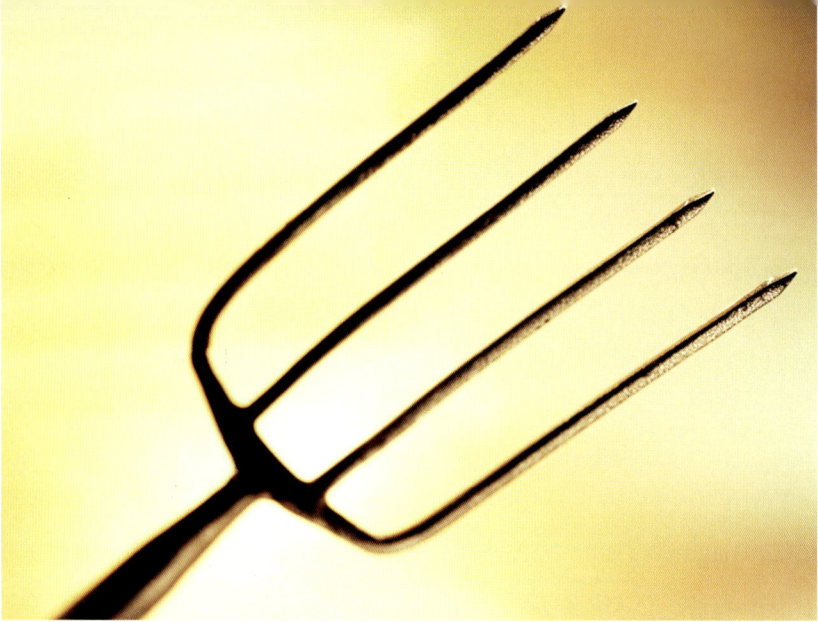

Pitchforks are often associated with images of the devil.

This **urban legend** is just one of thousands of sightings of the devil. Typically, the devil is described by witnesses as having small horns jutting from his head and a sharp, arrow-shaped tail. His weapon of choice is a three-pointed pitchfork.

Known by many names—Satan, Lucifer, the Prince of Darkness, Old Scratch—this ancient being is thought to embody all that is truly evil in the world. Although sightings are rare, for many the devil's presence is a powerful and dangerous one. Those who claim to have seen him say it is an experience they will never forget.

Fallen Angel

Judeo-Christian **theology** says that Satan started life as an angel—God's favorite, in fact. The Torah, an ancient Hebrew text, does not portray Satan as an evil spirit. Instead, he is God's spy who carefully watches humans and reports their misdeeds to his master.

More commonly, Satan is thought to have craved more and more power, until he considered himself greater than God. As punishment for Satan's disobedience, God cast him out of heaven and into the fires of hell to dwell there for eternity.

A Dreadful Place

This dark and desolate place is said to exist far below our feet. Sinful humans are sent there after they die. In hell, the devil and his minions (less powerful beings called demons) torture these souls for eternity.

No firsthand accounts of hell exist, but writers throughout the centuries have imagined it. In the

The Devil and the Queen

In 1953 Queen Elizabeth II took the British throne. A year later, all of the empire's money was reprinted with the new monarch's image. But the bank notes soon caused a stir. People noticed something strange about the young queen's hair: a grinning devil behind her ear. This "devil's face" series was discontinued in 1956. How it got there in the first place remains a mystery.

14th century, Italian poet Dante Alighieri provided perhaps the most famous description. In his epic poem *The Divine Comedy,* he wrote the "Darkness of Hell and of night deprived/Of every planet under a poor sky."[3] In Dante's *Inferno*, a sign at the entrance to hell reads, "All hope abandon, ye who enter here."[4]

In 1741 religious leader Jonathan Edwards offered his vision of this dreadful place. Eternal punishment awaited those who did not repent their sins: "The devil is waiting for them," he said. "Hell is gaping for them, the flames gather and flash about them."[5]

More recently, movies and TV shows have portrayed hell in similar ways, sometimes playing it for laughs. Even the animated show *The Simpsons* got into the act. In a 1995 episode, Homer Simpson is doomed to hell over a devilish donut.

Signs of the Devil

The most common signs of the devil include chicken feet or cloven hooves—since the devil at times disguises himself as an animal. His **diabolical** presence is suggested in folklore by black cats; strange, unexplained noises; and demonic possession. In possession, a human is taken over—body and mind—by a destructive and unearthly presence.

Also significant is the mark of the beast—the number 666. Superstitious people will often shy away from this number, even when it appears on their driver's license or a bar code on a can of corn in the supermarket.

The devil is capable of disguising himself as an animal, and he sometimes takes the form of a black cat.

Hunting the Jersey Devil

New Jersey residents have witnessed strange signs for hundreds of years. Those living near the eerie Pine Barrens are especially vulnerable. That is because these vast and tangled miles of trees are home to the legendary Jersey Devil.

In November 2004 a teenager on a nighttime walk with his younger brother came face-to-face with the mysterious creature. He is still amazed they lived to tell about it.

"We were about to walk away when we heard a horrible screeching noise," he said. "We turned around and the thing we had thought was a person was . . . only fifteen feet away. Its wings were spread out and it was looking straight at us."[6] They saw something, and they were certain of one thing: it was not human.

The Jersey Devil is thought to live in the miles of trees that make up Pine Barrens, New Jersey.

As legend has it, in 1735 Mrs. Leeds of Smithville, New Jersey, was giving birth to her thirteenth child on a dark and stormy night. Leeds, tired from all of her previous labors, cursed her new infant. "Let this child be the devil!"[7] she said. Soon after, her beautiful new boy began changing into a hideous, batlike creature, with wings and hooves. The baby's blue eyes turned a watery yellow. It let out a terrible scream, crashed through the roof of the family cabin, and escaped.

Today devil hunters have made it their mission to spot or catch this shadowy creature, but thus far it has remained **elusive**. For them, the search for signs of the devil's presence continues.

Does the Devil Exist?

Most modern historians argue that the devil is not an actual being. They describe it as a way of understanding terrible events. The devil, they say, is just the explanation people give to things they do not understand.

But tell that to the group of men who were playing cards one evening by the light of a kerosene lamp. After many hours of laughter the friends were in a good mood. Then there came a loud knock on the cabin door.

One of the men answered it, and in stepped a tall, dark stranger. He was cold and hungry, he told them, and asked if he could join them for the night.

The men welcomed him to stay and play a hand of cards. Before long, the stranger was winning all

Jersey and the Devil: Perfect Together

New Jersey has more people per square mile than any other state in the United States. So it may be hard to imagine how the Jersey Devil has never been caught. But like the Loch Ness Monster or Big Foot, stories of the Jersey Devil likely persist because legends are fun to talk about. They also help sell T-shirts.

of their money. After a time, one man dropped a jack of hearts on the floor. When he bent down he saw the stranger's feet—cloven hooves. Terrified, the man stood up and knocked over the table and the kerosene lamp, which set the cabin ablaze.

The devil resides in hell with his minions, less powerful beings known as demons.

What's in a Name?

Various cultures and religions have their own versions of the devil. Muslims call their Satanic figure Iblis. Ancient Persians referred to the powers of good (Ahura Mazda) and evil (Angra Mainyu). Norse mythology tells of Loki, the trickster. Whatever its name or origin, this creature typically has one job: to lead humans into sin.

Leaving their guest behind, the men rushed outside and took shelter under a tree until sunrise. When they awoke, they found no sign of the stranger. All that was left was "their silver money melted into an upside down cross"[8]—a sign of the devil.

Such stories persist, despite the skeptics. All that is seen and experienced cannot be explained. For many, the devil walks among us, and nothing will convince them otherwise.

Chapter 2

DISGUISED AND DANGEROUS

Countless stories detail the devil's existence. In most of them, the evil one lurks in forests or appears when and where he is least expected. Typically the devil is disguised, dressed like the rest of us, or comes in the form of an animal. He charms those he meets and then tempts his victims with a reward. His offer may include money, power, knowledge, or long life. In return, he asks for only one thing: his victims' souls.

Adam, Eve, and the Apple

One of the oldest stories in Western culture concerns the first man and first woman and their disastrous meeting with the devil. It is not known exactly who

these people were or when they lived, but the Old Testament calls them Adam and Eve. Adam was made in the image of God and ruled the beasts of the earth and the fish of the sea. Eve, so we are told, was created from one of Adam's ribs.

These two humans dwelled in a paradise called the Garden of Eden. Here, Adam and Eve lived life without a care. The garden is yours, God told them, all except for a special tree—the Tree of Knowledge. This they were not to touch.

Adam and Eve lived in a beautiful paradise called the Garden of Eden.

But temptation is hard to fight. Before long, a serpent arrived on the scene. The Bible describes this slithery snake (really the devil in disguise) as crafty and subtle, which means he was expert at getting his way.

The serpent first talked to Eve. Try the fruit from the tree, he suggested. Not only is it tasty, but if you eat it "your eyes shall be opened."[9]

Eve knew she was not supposed to eat from the Tree of Knowledge, but the temptation was too strong, and the serpent could talk a good game. Eve took a bite of what might have been an apple, grape, or fig, and loved it. She gave some to Adam and he enjoyed it too. Maybe the devil made them do it, but they had disobeyed God.

The devil, disguised as a serpent, tempted Eve into eating the forbidden fruit from the Tree of Knowledge.

Snake Down

While western tradition portrays the serpent as evil and crafty, the Chinese concept of this reptile is different. In China, the ancient wisdom of Feng Shui teaches that one potent symbol of good luck is the head of a snake.

Adam and Eve were ashamed. In his anger, God cast them out of the beautiful garden. The devil had won the day.

Faust Wants to Know

No one will ever know if Adam and Eve really existed. A more recent legend—this one clearly based in fact—also shows the devil's use of craft and persuasion.

A man named Faust was born sometime in the 15th century—historians think around 1480. His fellow Germans knew him as a magician and psychic. Reports also hint that he was a schoolteacher who traveled the countryside performing illusions and telling fortunes.

In time, Faust gained the respect of his country-men, including a powerful archbishop. But it is here that fact and fiction gets fuzzy. Rumors spread that Faust's magical skills came from a **pact** he made with the devil.

The magician known as Faust makes a pact with the devil.

Did Faust gain knowledge and power by selling his soul? Had the devil tricked him into an unfair trade? No one knows for sure.

Since then, the Faust legend has been retold countless times. In all versions of the story, the brilliant magician knows right from wrong, but he cannot help himself. His desire for knowledge and power is just too strong. He trades his soul to live his dream.

Robert Johnson and the Blues

Most would consider the devil's bargain a terrible choice, but some stories suggest that people will do foolish things to live their dreams. The devil, it seems, followed Robert Johnson from an early age. Johnson was born in Hazlehurst, Mississippi, on May 8, 1911. In his early teens, he began to take an interest in music.

The blues was Johnson's bread and butter. He understood this music deep down in his heart.

Friends say that Johnson could hear a song over the radio just once and be able to play it himself.

Johnson's talent as a singer, songwriter, and guitarist was so amazing that people wondered where he had learned to play so well. As the years went on, rumors began to swirl. Johnson never denied them.

One evening, Robert Johnson met the devil at a crossroads. It was getting on to midnight when Satan walked up to Johnson, took the young man's guitar, and tuned it. Then the devil played a song, handed it back to Johnson, and made his offer: Johnson's soul for the ability to play like Lucifer himself.

Today Robert Johnson is considered one of the greatest bluesmen ever. But the devil claimed his soul early. In 1938 Robert Johnson was poisoned

Blues guitarist Robert Johnson was said to have learned his craft from the devil.

for stealing another man's girlfriend. He was just 27 years old when he died. He left behind this song:

> I gotta keep movin'
> Blues fallin' down like hail
> And the days keep on worryin' me
> There's a hellhound on my trail.[10]

An Offer Refused

Unlike Robert Johnson and Faust, one notable historical figure said no to the devil despite the temptation. For Christians, the New Testament is the sacred section of the Bible that chronicles the life and teachings of Jesus Christ.

As a young adult, this holy man traveled throughout what we know today as the Middle East. He preached the word of God and told followers that

The Devil's Music

The blues was, perhaps, the first music form to be labeled the devil's music. But it was not the last. With the advent of rock and roll in the 1950s, recording artists like Elvis Presley, Jerry Lee Lewis, and later, the Rolling Stones and Led Zeppelin, were often accused of tempting young people into sin.

The devil tries but fails to persuade Jesus to display his power by jumping from the top of a mountain.

heaven was open to all who kept God's laws and loved one another.

The Gospel of Matthew describes the 40 days and 40 nights Jesus spent fasting in the wilderness. Because of Jesus's hunger and physical weakness, the devil sees an opportunity. Dressed like any other man of the time, Satan first asks Jesus to prove himself. "If thou be the Son of God," he said, "command that these stones be made bread." [11]

Jesus's famous response to the devil—"Man shall not live by bread alone" [12]—shows the inner strength of the man being tempted. But the devil—ever patient—is not easily defeated. He leads Jesus to a hilltop above the holy city of Jerusalem and tells Jesus to throw himself from the top of the temple to show his power. Again, Jesus rejects the devil. He has nothing to prove and will not be destroyed by pride.

Finally, the devil promises Jesus great power over "all the kingdoms of the world."[13] Surely this, the evil creature imagines, will win him Jesus's soul. But again, Jesus reveals his inner strength. He tells Satan to leave him alone, and by doing so defeats his mortal enemy.

Only Human

At one time or another, all people are tempted into inappropriate behavior. Human nature is designed to sometimes want what it cannot or should not have, but people will go to great lengths to achieve their desires. Stories about meeting the devil remind us that while temptation is natural, not every whim needs to be satisfied.

Chapter 3

Possessed by the Devil

The idea of meeting the devil is frightening enough. But in some cases, Satan may enter a person's body, causing frightening behavior and physical harm. This possession can last for days or months, while the victim writhes in pain and is controlled from the inside out. Stories of demonic possession are among the most horrifying stories of encounters people have with the devil.

The Salem Witch Trials

For Puritans in 17th-century New England, the devil was ever present. In fact, he lived in the forest that surrounded them. Children were warned to stay out of the woods, or else be led into sin and damnation.

These warnings did not stop eleven-year-old Abigail Williams. She, along with a number of other girls from Salem, Massachusetts, often ventured into the wilderness.

There a local slave woman named Tituba told them tales of Barbados, where she had grown up. She encouraged the girls to dance and play games. The girls' favorite was a fortune-telling game. By cracking eggs in water and "reading" them, the girls thought they could learn the names of future sweethearts.

All of this was strictly forbidden. The Puritans were a religious sect that believed in living a simple, sin-free life. They thought that God had a plan for

Girls are accused of possession by the devil during the Salem witch trials.

Witches' Brew

The events of Salem in 1692 remain shrouded in mystery. But one explanation for the girls' behavior is especially intriguing. Ergot, a fungus sometimes found in rye grain and used in bread, is known to cause hallucinations. Could the young women's strange actions have been a result of illness from food contamination?

each of them, but they also worried about spirits and the power of Lucifer.

Then Abigail Williams and the preacher's daughter, Betty Parris, began acting strangely. Sudden screaming, falling down, and wild contortions were common. The Parris family was alarmed and called in the local physician, Dr. Griggs. After a careful examination of Betty Parris, Griggs came to a stark conclusion: "The hand of evil is upon them."[14]

Word of the stricken girls spread quickly. Soon Salem was in a panic. The community's worst fears had become a reality. On February 29, 1692, the afflicted girls began accusing others of witchcraft. Local officials investigated, and before long, the infamous Salem witch trials were underway.

In the upside-down thinking of the time, if the accused person confessed he or she was released. If that person denied knowing the devil and signing his book, he or she would be jailed or hanged. This **hysteria** continued for months.

According to one court document, a woman named Mary Osgood "made a covenant with the devil, who came to her and presented her a book, upon which she laid a finger and . . . left a red spot."[15] Testimony like this only caused more fear among the Puritan leaders. As a result, local jails were overrun with accused witches. One was only three years old.

By the time the trials came to an end, fourteen women and five men had been hanged, one man was pressed to death between two heavy rocks, and four died in jail. In all almost 200 people had been arrested.

Today the Salem witch trials are recognized as a terrible mistake, but one question still remains: Were the girls who started them truly possessed by the devil?

Man of the Cloth

More recently, demonic possession was blamed in the strange case of a young man named Giancarlo. At the age of 25, Giancarlo was studying for the priesthood in Italy. He worked hard, prayed every day, and dedicated his life to serving God.

But over time, Giancarlo's behavior became unusual. Almost every night he would toss and turn in bed, sometimes violently. His family was frightened and did not know what to do. They were religious people and attended church every Sunday. Often they had listened to sermons about the battle be-

Church officials try to loosen the devil's hold through exorcism rituals.

tween good and evil. Yet at first they refused to believe that this same struggle might be going on under their own roof.

That is until Giancarlo got worse. His fits became more dreadful. He threw things around the room, turned over tables, and thrashed about like a wild animal. His five brothers often spent all night holding him down and keeping him calm.

Once, Giancarlo tried jumping out a window. Another time he smashed his hand through glass, badly injuring it. He screamed and growled like a ferocious tiger at anyone who entered his bedroom. Most terribly, Giancarlo was fully aware of what was happening to him. Although he bravely fought the evil within him, it seemed his body was no longer his own. It had been taken over by a powerful and destructive force. His torment was such that he became suicidal.

Possessed by the Devil   **27**

A local priest visited Giancarlo. He had witnessed such symptoms before and, after careful observation of the young man, made his diagnosis. "I was in the presence of total demonic possession,"[16] he said.

House of Horrors

One of the most notorious demonic possessions on record occurred in the small town of Amityville, New York, in 1975. In this case, the devil did not take over a person; instead, he possessed a whole house.

It began with a brutal murder. On November 13, 1974, Louise and Ronald DeFeo, as well as four of their children, were shot to death. Ron Jr., another son, was convicted of the crime and jailed. Soon after, the house was put up for sale.

Inhabitants of 112 Ocean Avenue, also known as the Amityville Horror house, believed the house was possessed by the devil.

Amityville Hoax?

In 1977 the book and movie versions of *The Amityville Horror* became huge hits. Since that time, the story has been questioned. Lawyer William Weber claims that he and the Lutzes made up the story for money and fame.

A year later, 112 Ocean Avenue was sold to George and Kathy Lutz. Almost immediately after the couple and their three children moved in, the nightmare began. Doors suddenly started opening and closing, green slime oozed from the ceilings, and a swarm of insects attacked the house. Most frightening of all were the red eyes that peered at the Lutzes through the windows at night and the cloven-hoof footprints they found in the snow almost every morning.

The Lutzes said they were living in a house of hell, and they had the evidence to prove it. Experts on the supernatural were called in and spent days investigating. Most of them agreed that the house was indeed possessed. One popular theory was that young Ron DeFeo had killed his family because the house had possessed him.

By the time Jay Anson's book *The Amityville Horror* was published in 1977, the Lutzes had moved far away from Amityville, never to return. What exactly happened in their house over that long winter has never been fully explained.

"Get Out and Let Him Alone"

Like the house of horrors in Amityville, the story of Robbie Manheim remains baffling. On January 15, 1949, Karl and Phyllis Manheim decided to have a night out. The couple left their young son, Robbie, in the care of his Grandmother Wagner. But the old woman soon began hearing a loud dripping sound.

The two went from room to room until Grandmother Wagner and the boy discovered something strange. A painting of Jesus in her room was shaking violently. By the time Robbie's parents re-

Exorcisms, like the one performed on Robbie Manheim, have been done since the time of Jesus.

turned, another unusual sound had started: the scratching of claws on the hard wood underneath Grandmother Wagner's bed.

Adding to the family's growing fright was Robbie's peculiar behavior. Like the Salem girls, he began throwing fits, hissing, and making other strange and unsettling noises. This was not the child they knew. The Manheim family called local minister Reverend Luther Schulze, who visited Robbie. "At first I tried to pray," he said. Then he ordered "whatever it was disturbing him, in the name of the Father, Son, and Holy Spirit, to get out and let him alone." [17]

Despite Schulze's efforts, this was only the beginning of Robbie Manheim's **ordeal**. What began as a case of odd childhood behavior would someday frighten millions.

Chapter 4

Exorcism and Exorcists

The only known cure for demonic possession is **exorcism**. This ancient ritual uses prayers and holy water to rid a person's body and mind of the devil. The Catholic Church performs a handful of exorcisms every year. Believers feel that only an exorcist can overcome the dark and fearsome hold Satan has on his victims. For Robbie Manheim, an exorcist was just what the devil did not order.

"Fight to the Finish"

Nothing in Luther Schulze's experience as a Lutheran minister had prepared him for what was happening to Robbie Manheim. On February 17, 1949, Robbie's father dropped the boy off at Schulze's house. The reverend wanted to observe his weird behavior more closely.

At midnight Schulze was woken by the sound of Robbie's shaking bed. Schulze offered Robbie some hot chocolate and had the boy sleep in a bedroom chair. The chair, too, began moving.

"'Stop that,' Schulze shouted at Robbie. 'I'm not doing it,' said the boy."[18]

Over the following weeks, Robbie's condition became more disturbing. A heavy bookcase in Robbie's house suddenly moved. He answered his parents' questions using a sinister voice not his own.

The story of Robbie Manheim was one of many tales that told of the devil possessing the souls of children.

His mattress shook more violently than ever. Schulze was **baffled**. He knew he could not manage on his own.

A Jesuit priest named Father Bowdern was contacted to help release Robbie from this bond of evil. Around the clock, the priest recited prayers over the boy's bed: "Let the enemy have no power over him," he said. "Send him, Lord, aid from on high." [19] Many days and nights passed, and Robbie's condition worsened. More prayer and ritual followed, with no end in sight.

Then a ray of light appeared. Robbie's symptoms gradually lessened. Bowdern's methods, it seemed, were beginning to work. Still, it was not easy, and a cure was not assured.

A bishop familiar with the case called the last days of the exorcism a "fight to the finish." [20] But finally, the screaming and torment of Robbie Manheim stopped. In time, with rest and prayer, the boy was rid of the devil.

In 1973 a movie based on Robbie's chilling experience was released. *The Exorcist,* about a little girl possessed by the devil and the priest who saves her, became a worldwide hit. To this day, many moviegoers call it the scariest movie ever made.

The Stages of Exorcism

Perhaps the foremost expert on exorcisms like Robbie Manheim's is former priest Malachi Martin. In 1976 Martin published the best-selling book *Hostage to the Devil.* In it, he interviewed many former victims of demonic possession.

Through his research, Martin was able to conclude that the ritual of exorcism consists of four distinct stages. First comes a phase called pretense, in which the demon disguises his true identity from the exorcist. Next is the breakpoint, where the evil one gives up his trickery and speaks in his own voice. This is followed by clash, the stage in which the devil and the exorcist battle for the soul of the possessed. Finally, there is the expulsion stage, where the demon is cast out of the victim.

One supporter of Martin's exorcism work was M. Scott Peck, a famous psychiatrist. Although Peck prided himself on reason over belief, one experience with a troubled patient convinced him that exorcism was sometimes a legitimate last resort. Peck once described this patient's satanic grin. "The patient resembled a writhing snake," he said. Peck was convinced that only through exorcism could his disturbed patient be cured. This dreadful episode convinced Peck that "the role of exorcist was a heroic one."[21]

Expulsion

For Giancarlo, the possessed seminary student, heroism was badly needed. Expulsion could not

Priests perform exorcisms by reciting prayers, sprinkling holy water, and commanding the devil to leave the body of the afflicted person.

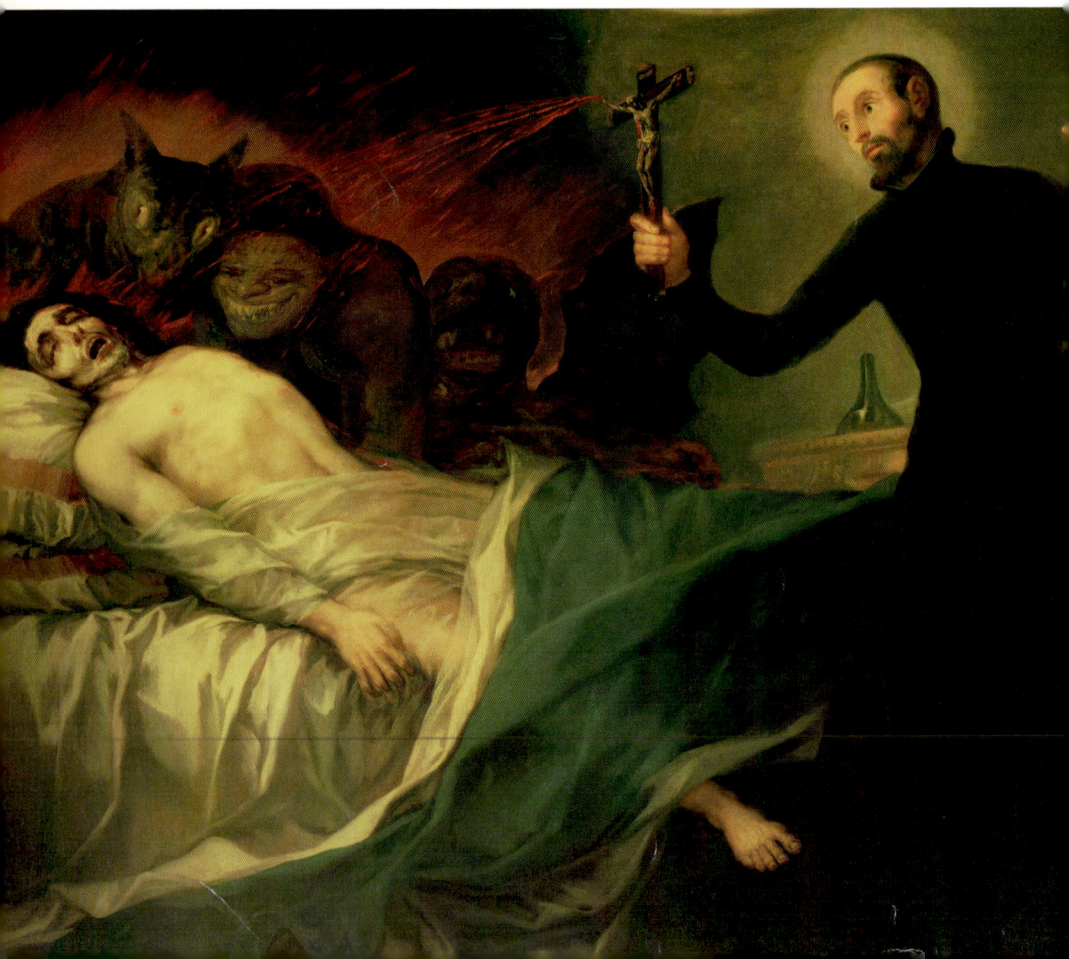

come soon enough. Over many long nights, Father Gabriele Amorth stood over Giancarlo's bed. He recited prayers, sprinkled holy water, and told the devil to be gone. It did not work.

A psychiatrist was summoned and declared that Giancarlo was hysterical, not possessed. A vacation was what he needed, said the psychiatrist. But the young man's violence continued.

Desperate for a remedy, a second psychiatrist examined Giancarlo. This one declared the young man's mind normal and not in need of counseling or vacation. Upon hearing this, Amorth renewed his attempts to cast out the devil and became determined not to give up.

After three long years of weekly visits from this dedicated priest, Giancarlo found peace. "The Lord lavished his graces on him,"[22] said Amorth. Giancarlo, after great suffering, was finally back to normal.

"I Exorcise You"

To hear Ed Warren tell it, normal is a relative term. After years of "boredom and curiosity,"[23] he began leading a life full of alcohol and parties. He became a prisoner to his own bad behavior and saw no way out.

After watching a news program about a possessed teenager named Gina, he got the idea that exorcism was the only way to change his life. With his decision made, Warren hired a priest named Father Peter to perform the ritual.

Father Peter began the exorcism by standing above Warren's bed and making the sign of the cross. He sprinkled holy water on Warren and spoke. "Pardon all of the sins of your unworthy servant." The priest again made the sign of the cross and put a hand on Warren's head. "I exorcise you, Most Unclean Spirit,"[24] said Father Peter.

All was calm as Father Peter pressed a religious **relic**—a small splinter of wood—into Warren's bare chest. More prayers followed, as did Warren's shouts of pain. The devil, if he was in there, would not go quietly.

After many hours, the exorcism ended with Father Peter shouting, "Go away, Seducer! The devil is your home."[25] Warren was conscious now, and

Jesus drives a demon out of a man who is possessed.

Repulsive Regan

The movie *The Exorcist* was talked about, in part, because it left so little to the imagination. One famous sequence shows the possessed girl's head turning 360 degrees. In another, she spits a green globule and speaks in a deep voice. Was it really possession or just a bad head cold? Sometimes Hollywood makes it hard to tell the difference.

the priest led him in a number of prayers. He asked Warren how he was feeling.

Warren did not answer right away. He was confused but quiet. He claims that during the exorcism he felt something leave his body but he could not be sure. He would never be quite sure.

The Search Goes On

Regardless of time and place, encounters with the devil will no doubt continue. Still, Satan—if he is really out there—remains hard to pin down. One religious official argues, "He's a creation of man."[26] But Roman Catholicism, especially, believes in the physical reality of Satan. People will never know whether the devil lives only in the hearts of those

A priest and exorcist of the Roman Catholic Church displays the church's official book of exorcism rituals and prayers.

who give in to the dark side of life. They will never know if he really makes contact with the human world from time to time through demonic possession. What is clear is that people will continue looking for him by asking questions and trying to get to the bottom of evil in our world.

Notes

Chapter 1: Signs of the Devil

1. Quoted in Urban Legend Reference Pages, Snopes.com, "Satan's Choice," January 16, 2007. www.snopes.com/horrors/ghosts/devil.asp.
2. Quoted in Urban Legend Reference Pages, Snopes.com, "Satan's Choice."
3. Quoted in Dante Alighieri, *The Divine Comedy of Dante Alighieri.* New York: Columbia University Press, 1931, p. 17.
4. Quoted in Alighieri, *The Divine Comedy,* p. 12.
5. Quoted in Jonathan Edwards, *The Sermons of Jonathan Edwards: A Reader.* New Haven and London: Yale University Press, 1999, p. 55.
6. Quoted in The Devil Hunters, "The Pine Barrens Chase." www.njdevilhunters.com/pers2004 d.html.
7. Quoted in Laura Leuter, "The Legend of the Jersey Devil," The Devil Hunters. www.njdevil hunters.com/legend.html.
8. Quoted in Urban Legend Reference Pages, Snopes.com, "Satan's Choice."

Chapter 2: Disguised and Dangerous

9. Quoted in *The Holy Bible: King James Version.* Camden, NJ: Thomas Nelson, p. 7.
10. Quoted in Music and Media International, "Hellhound on My Trail." www.deltahaze.com/ johnson/lyrics.html.

11. Quoted in *The Holy Bible*, p. 5.
12. Quoted in *The Holy Bible*, p. 5.
13. Quoted in *The Holy Bible*, p. 5.

Chapter 3: Possessed by the Devil

14. Quoted in Jane Yolen and Heidi Elisabet Yolen Stemple, *The Salem Witch Trials: An Unsolved Mystery from History*. New York/London: Simon & Schuster, 2004, p. 11.
15. Quoted in University of Virginia, "The Salem Witchcraft Papers: Verbatim Transcripts of the Legal Documents of the Salem Witchcraft Outbreak of 1692." http://etext.virginia.edu/salem/witchcraft/texts/transcripts.html.
16. Quoted in Gabriele Amorth, *An Exorcist: More Stories*. San Francisco: Ignatius, 2002, p. 83.
17. Quoted in Thomas B. Allen, *Possessed: The True Story of an Exorcism*. New York/London: Doubleday, 1993, p. 15.

Chapter 4: Exorcism and Exorcists

18. Quoted in Allen, *Possessed*, p. 21.
19. Quoted in Allen, *Possessed*, p. 174.
20. Quoted in Allen, *Possessed*, p. 192.
21. Quoted in Michael W. Cuneo, *American Exorcism: Expelling Demons in the Land of Plenty*. New York/London: Doubleday, 2001, p. 45.
22. Quoted in Amorth, *An Exorcist*, p. 84.
23. Quoted in Cuneo, *American Exorcism*, p. 242.
24. Quoted in Cuneo, *American Exorcism*, p. 243.
25. Quoted in Cuneo, *American Exorcism*, p. 243.
26. Quoted in Pamela Miller, "Who Is Satan?" *Star Tribune (Metro)*, March 18, 2006, p. 12E.

Glossary

baffled: Confused or not understanding.

diabolical: Evil.

elusive: Hard to find or catch.

exorcism: The process of casting out the devil or a demon.

hysteria: Extreme and uncontrollable excitement.

ordeal: A difficult or painful experience.

pact: An agreement.

relic: A historic object or artifact believed to be holy.

theology: The academic study of religion.

urban legend: A story that may or may not be true.

For Further Exploration

Books and Periodicals

Lauren Janis, "Jersey Devil Hunters Insist the Beast Exists," *Burlington County Times*, October 31, 2004. This article attests to the popularity and mystery surrounding the Jersey Devil and the dedicated people who hunt for it.

Jane Yolen and Heidi Elisabet Yolen Stemple. *The Salem Witch Trials: An Unsolved Mystery from History*. New York/London: Simon & Schuster, 2004. Provides an introduction to the infamous witch trials and is told in a clear, straightforward manner. This complex subject is made much simpler by the use of child-friendly notes and illustrations.

Web Sites

New Jersey Devil Hunters (www.njdevilhunters.com). Those interested in learning more about the Jersey Devil and those who hunt it will find fascinating information here, including firsthand accounts of meeting the devil, a complete history of the legend, and newspaper reports of sighting.

Salem Witchcraft Papers (http://etext.virginia.edu/ salem). Edited by two historians, this site provides the entire transcript of the Salem witch trials of

1692–1693. It is chock-full of historical documents and other information.

Urban Legends Reference Pages, Snopes.com (www.snopes.com). This is an amazing Web site for all those interested in exploring what to believe and what not to. Started by university professors, Snopes is regularly updated, and legends are investigated on a regular basis.

Index

About the Author

David Robson is a playwright, freelance writer, and English professor. His work has been presented from Florida to Alaska and places in between. David was a recent playwright in residence at the Lark Theatre Company in New York City, and he is the recipient of an NEA grant and two playwriting fellowships from the Delaware Division of the Arts. When he was eight, he dressed as the devil for Halloween and scared his Aunt Betty half to death. David lives in Wilmington, Delaware, with his two angels, wife Sonja and daughter Ingrid. This is his first book for KidHaven Press.